THE WIT AND WISDOM OF WILLIAM SHAKESPEARE

Max Morris

THE WIT AND WISDOM OF WILLIAM SHAKESPEARE

First published in 2014 as *Quotable Shakespeare*

Reprinted 2015

Summersdale Publishers Ltd
46 West Street
Chichester
West Sussex
PO19 1RP
UK

www.summersdale.com

Printed and bound in the Czech Republic

ISBN: 978-1-84953-855-8

Substantial discounts on bulk quantities of Summersdale books are available to corporations, professional associations and other organisations. For details contact Nicky Douglas by telephone: +44 (0) 1243 756902, fax: +44 (0) 1243 786300 or email: nicky@summersdale.com.

THE **WIT** AND **WISDOM** OF **WILLIAM** SHAKESPEARE

Max Morris

summersdale

CONTENTS

LOVE'S LIGHT WINGS

Doubt thou the stars are fire;
Doubt that the sun doth move;
Doubt truth to be a liar;
But never doubt I love.

POLONIUS, READING HAMLET'S
LETTER TO OPHELIA, *HAMLET*

Love is a spirit all compact of fire.

VENUS AND ADONIS

With love's light wings did I
o'er-perch these walls;
For stony limits cannot hold love out.

ROMEO, *ROMEO AND JULIET*

Shall I compare thee
to a summer's day?
Thou art more lovely
and more temperate.

SONNET 18

Eternity was in our lips and eyes.

CLEOPATRA, *ANTONY AND CLEOPATRA*

But soft, what light through
yonder window breaks?
It is the east, and Juliet is the sun.

ROMEO, *ROMEO AND JULIET*

All days are nights to
see, till I see thee,
And nights, bright days,
when dreams do
Show thee me.

SONNET 43

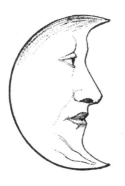

Good night, good night!
Parting is such sweet sorrow
That I shall say good
night till it be morrow.

JULIET, *ROMEO AND JULIET*

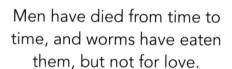

Men have died from time to
time, and worms have eaten
them, but not for love.

ROSALIND, *AS YOU LIKE IT*

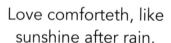

Love comforteth, like
sunshine after rain.

VENUS AND ADONIS

Love alters not with his
brief hours and weeks,
But bears it out even to
the edge of doom.

SONNET 116

———◆———

Love sought is good, but
given unsought is better.

OLIVIA, *TWELFTH NIGHT*

———◆———

Not marble, nor the gilded monuments
Of princes, shall outlive this
powerful rhyme;
But you shall shine more
bright in these contents.

SONNET 55

Love is a smoke raised
with the fume of sighs;
Being purged, a fire
sparkling in lovers' eyes.

ROMEO, *ROMEO AND JULIET*

My bounty is as boundless as the sea,
My love as deep; the more I give to thee,
The more I have, for both are infinite.

JULIET, *ROMEO AND JULIET*

———◆———

The sight of lovers feedeth
those in love.

ROSALIND, *AS YOU LIKE IT*

———◆———

And when love speaks, the
voice of all the gods
Makes heaven drowsy
with the harmony.

BIRON, *LOVE'S LABOUR'S LOST*

One half of me is yours,
the other half yours,
Mine own, I would say;
but if mine, then yours,
And so all yours.

PORTIA, *THE MERCHANT OF VENICE*

O, she doth teach the
torches to burn bright.

ROMEO, *ROMEO AND JULIET*

———◆———

This is the very ecstasy of love,
Whose violent property fordoes itself,
And leads the will to
desperate undertakings.

POLONIUS, *HAMLET*

———◆———

Love is not love,
Which alters when it alteration finds.

SONNET 116

You have witchcraft in your lips.

KING HENRY, *THE LIFE OF KING HENRY V*

So, till the judgement that yourself arise,
You live in this, and dwell
in lovers' eyes.

SONNET 55

The course of true love
never did run smooth.

LYSANDER, *A MIDSUMMER NIGHT'S DREAM*

But here's the joy; my friend and I are one;
Sweet flattery! Then she
loves but me alone.

SONNET 42

FORTUNE'S WHEEL

Now is the winter
of our discontent
Made glorious summer
by this son of York;
And all the clouds that
loured upon our house
In the deep bosom of
the ocean buried.

RICHARD, DUKE OF GLOUCESTER,
THE TRAGEDY OF KING RICHARD III

There is seen the baby
figure of the giant mass
Of things to come.

NESTOR, *TROILUS AND CRESSIDA*

———◆———

Thy end is truth's and beauty's
doom and date.

SONNET 14

———◆———

My fate cries out,
And makes each petty artery in this body
As hardy as the Nemean lion's nerve.

HAMLET, *HAMLET*

Giddy Fortune's furious
fickle wheel,
That goddess blind,
That stands upon the
rolling restless stone.

PISTOL, *THE LIFE OF KING HENRY V*

O, I am fortune's fool!

ROMEO, *ROMEO AND JULIET*

———◆———

Our remedies oft in ourselves do lie,
Which we ascribe to heaven: the fated sky.

HELENA, *ALL'S WELL THAT ENDS WELL*

———◆———

If it be now, 'tis not to come; if it be not
to come, it will be now; if it be not now,
yet it will come: the readiness is all.

HAMLET, *HAMLET*

When Fortune means to
men most good,
She looks upon them with
a threatening eye.

CARDINAL PANDULPH,
THE LIFE AND DEATH OF KING JOHN

If chance will have me king, why,
Chance may crown me.

MACBETH, *MACBETH*

Fortune brings in some boats,
that are not steer'd.

PISANIO, *CYMBELINE*

O God! That one might
read the book of fate,
And see the revolution
of the times.

KING HENRY, *THE SECOND PART OF
KING HENRY IV*

Men at some time are
masters of their fates:
The fault, dear Brutus,
is not in our stars,
But in ourselves, that we
are underlings.

CASSIUS, *JULIUS CAESAR*

What fates impose, that
men must needs abide;
It boots not to resist both
wind and tide.

KING EDWARD, *THE THIRD PART OF
KING HENRY VI*

The stars above us govern
our conditions.

EARL OF KENT, *KING LEAR*

There's a divinity that shapes our ends,
Rough-hew them how we will.

HAMLET, *HAMLET*

Think you, I bear the shears of destiny?
Have I commandment on the pulse of life?

KING JOHN, *THE LIFE AND DEATH OF KING JOHN*

Out, out, thou strumpet,
Fortune! All you gods,
In general synod take away her power.

FIRST PLAYER, *HAMLET*

As flies to wanton boys,
are we to the gods;
They kill us for their sport.

EARL OF GLOUCESTER, *KING LEAR*

GO
WISELY
AND SLOW

When sorrows come, they
come not single spies,
But in battalions.

CLAUDIUS, *HAMLET*

———◆———

Blow, blow, thou winter wind,
Thou art not so unkind
As man's ingratitude.

AMIENS, *AS YOU LIKE IT*

———◆———

Our doubts are traitors,
And make us lose the good
we oft might win
By fearing to attempt.

LUCIO, *MEASURE FOR MEASURE*

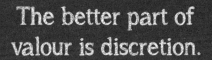

The better part of
valour is discretion.

FALSTAFF,
THE FIRST PART OF KING HENRY IV

The fool doth think he is wise, but the wise man knows himself to be a fool.

TOUCHSTONE, *AS YOU LIKE IT*

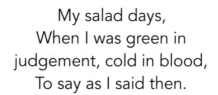

My salad days,
When I was green in
judgement, cold in blood,
To say as I said then.

CLEOPATRA, *ANTONY AND CLEOPATRA*

If you prick us, do we not bleed? If you tickle us, do we not laugh? If you poison us, do we not die? And if you wrong us, shall we not revenge?

SHYLOCK, *THE MERCHANT OF VENICE*

Ignorance is the
curse of God,
Knowledge the
wing wherewith we
fly to heaven.

SAY, *THE SECOND PART OF KING HENRY VI*

Wisely and slow, they
stumble that run fast.

FRIAR LAWRENCE, *ROMEO AND JULIET*

———◆———

Give every man thy ear,
but few thy voice.

POLONIUS, *HAMLET*

———◆———

It is a wise father, that
knows his own child.

LAUNCELOT GOBBO, *THE MERCHANT OF VENICE*

The common curse
of mankind, folly
and ignorance.

THERSITES, *TROILUS AND CRESSIDA*

Nothing will come of nothing.

KING LEAR, *KING LEAR*

———◆———

Tempt not a desperate man.

ROMEO, *ROMEO AND JULIET*

———◆———

Words, without thoughts,
never to heaven go.

CLAUDIUS, *HAMLET*

Suspicion always haunts the guilty mind.

RICHARD, DUKE OF GLOUCESTER, *THE THIRD PART OF KING HENRY VI*

Things without all remedy
Should be without regard;
what's done is done.

LADY MACBETH, *MACBETH*

———◆———

Action is eloquence.

VOLUMNIA, *CORIOLANUS*

———◆———

Live a little; comfort a little;
cheer thyself a little.

ORLANDO, *AS YOU LIKE IT*

GET THEE A WIFE OR HUSBAND

Let me not to the marriage of true minds
Admit impediments.

SONNET 116

Rosalind: Now tell me, how
long you would have her after
you have possessed her.
Orlando: For ever and a day.

AS YOU LIKE IT

Who wooed in haste and
means to wed at leisure.

KATHERINA, *THE TAMING OF THE SHREW*

Marriage is a matter
of more worth
Than to be dealt in
by attorneyship.

EARL OF SUFFOLK,
THE FIRST PART OF KING HENRY VI

If men could be contented
to be what they are, there
were no fear in marriage.

CLOWN, *ALL'S WELL THAT ENDS WELL*

Men are April when they woo,
December when they wed.

ROSALIND, *AS YOU LIKE IT*

The fittest time to corrupt a
man's wife is when she's fallen
out with her husband.

ROMAN, *CORIOLANUS*

A young man married is a man that's marr'd.

PAROLLES, *ALL'S WELL THAT ENDS WELL*

Thou art sad; get thee a
wife, get thee a wife.

BENEDICK TO DON PEDRO,
MUCH ADO ABOUT NOTHING

—◆—

O, curse of marriage!
That we can call these
delicate creatures ours,
And not their appetites!

OTHELLO, *OTHELLO*

—◆—

What's mine is yours, and
what is yours is mine.

VINCENTIO, *MEASURE FOR MEASURE*

For what is wedlock
forced but a hell.

EARL OF SUFFOLK, *THE FIRST PART OF
KING HENRY VI*

———◆———

Get thee a good husband, and
use him as he uses thee.

PAROLLES, *ALL'S WELL THAT ENDS WELL*

———◆———

They shall be married tomorrow, and
I will bid the duke to the nuptial. But,
O, how bitter a thing it is to look into
happiness through another man's eyes!

ORLANDO, *AS YOU LIKE IT*

Many a good
hanging prevents
a bad marriage.

FESTE, *TWELFTH NIGHT*

What should such a fool
Do with so good a wife?

EMILIA, *OTHELLO*

———◆———

Wife and child,
Those precious motives, those
strong knots of love.

MALCOLM, *MACBETH*

———◆———

And kiss me, Kate, we will
be married o' Sunday.

PETRUCHIO, *THE TAMING OF THE SHREW*

TH'ABUSE OF GREATNESS

Therefore doth heaven divide
The state of man in divers functions.

ARCHBISHOP OF CANTERBURY,
THE LIFE OF KING HENRY V

———◆———

The smallest worm will turn,
being trodden on.

CLIFFORD, *THE THIRD PART OF KING HENRY VI*

———◆———

Power into will, will into appetite.

ULYSSES, *TROILUS AND CRESSIDA*

Man, proud man,
Drest in a little
brief authority,
Most ignorant of what
he's most assured.

ISABELLA, *MEASURE FOR MEASURE*

King Lear: Thou hast seen a farmer's dog bark at a beggar?
Earl of Gloucester: Ay, sir.
King Lear: And the creature run from the cur? There thou might'st behold the great image of authority: a dog's obeyed in office.

KING LEAR

— ◆ —

And though authority be a stubborn bear, yet he is oft led by the nose with gold.

CLOWN, *THE WINTER'S TALE*

— ◆ —

There is no fettering of authority.

PAROLLES, *ALL'S WELL THAT ENDS WELL*

Thus can the
demigod Authority
Make us pay down for
our offence by weight.

CLAUDIO, *MEASURE FOR MEASURE*

And, by his light,
Did all the chivalry of England move
To do brave acts.

**LADY PERCY, *THE SECOND PART OF
KING HENRY IV***

Reputation, reputation,
reputation! O, I have lost
my reputation! I have lost the
immortal part of myself.

CASSIO, *OTHELLO*

In the corrupted currents of this world
Offence's gilded hand may
shove by justice.

CLAUDIUS, *HAMLET*

Bell, book and candle
shall not drive me back,
When gold and silver
becks me to come on.

PHILIP FAULCONBRIDGE, *THE LIFE AND
DEATH OF KING JOHN*

Some are born great, some
achieve greatness, and some have
greatness thrust upon them.

MALVOLIO, *TWELFTH NIGHT*

———◆———

The heavens themselves, the
planets and this centre
Observe degree, priority and place.

ULYSSES, *TROILUS AND CRESSIDA*

———◆———

Th' abuse of greatness
is when it disjoins
Remorse from power.

BRUTUS, *JULIUS CAESAR*

Nay, had I power, I should
Pour the sweet milk of
concord into hell,
Uproar the universal
peace, confound
All unity on earth.

MALCOLM, *MACBETH*

Service is no heritage.

CLOWN, *ALL'S WELL THAT ENDS WELL*

———◆———

'Tis time to fear when
tyrants seem to kiss.

PERICLES, *PERICLES*

———◆———

There's place, and means,
for every man alive.

PAROLLES, *ALL'S WELL THAT ENDS WELL*

TIME, THAT OLD ARBITRATOR

Cowards die many times
before their deaths;
The valiant never taste
of death but once.

CAESAR, *JULIUS CAESAR*

———◆———

To weep is to make less
the depth of grief.

RICHARD, DUKE OF GLOUCESTER, *THE THIRD
PART OF KING HENRY VI*

———◆———

When we are born, we cry
that we are come
To this great stage of fools.

KING LEAR, *KING LEAR*

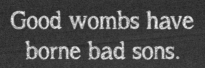

Good wombs have
borne bad sons.

MIRANDA, *THE TEMPEST*

To die, to sleep
To sleep, perchance to dream.

HAMLET, *HAMLET*

———◆———

Here's the smell of blood still:
all the perfumes of Arabia will
not sweeten this little hand.

LADY MACBETH, *MACBETH*

———◆———

The miserable have no other medicine,
But only hope.

CLAUDIO, *MEASURE FOR MEASURE*

Defer no time, delays have dangerous ends.

DUKE OF ALENÇON, *THE FIRST PART OF KING HENRY VI*

Now cracks a noble heart.
Goodnight sweet prince;
And flights of angels sing
thee to thy rest.

HORATIO, *HAMLET*

———◆———

'Tis a vile thing to die,
my gracious lord,
When men are unprepared
and look not for it.

WILLIAM CATESBY, *THE TRAGEDY OF
KING RICHARD III*

———◆———

The end crowns all;
And that old common arbitrator, time,
Will one day end it.

HECTOR, *TROILUS AND CRESSIDA*

This youth that you see here,
I snatched one-half out of
the jaws of death.

ANTONIO, *TWELFTH NIGHT*

———◆———

Nothing in his life
Became him, like the leaving it.

MALCOLM ON CAWDOR, *MACBETH*

———◆———

When it pleaseth their deities to take
the wife of a man from him, it shows to
man the tailors of the earth; comforting
therein, that when old robes are worn
out, there are members to make new.

ENOBARBUS, *ANTONY AND CLEOPATRA*

Is this a dagger which
I see before me,
The handle toward
my hand? Come, let
me clutch thee.

MACBETH, *MACBETH*

What's gone and what's past help
Should be past grief.

PAULINA, *THE WINTER'S TALE*

He that dies pays all debts.

STEPHANO, *THE TEMPEST*

How oft when men are at
the point of death
Have they been merry!
Which their keepers call
A lightning before death.

ROMEO, *ROMEO AND JULIET*

WE,
ARRANT
KNAVES

But, if it be a sin to covet honour,
I am the most offending soul alive.

KING HENRY, *THE LIFE OF KING HENRY V*

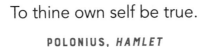

To thine own self be true.

POLONIUS, *HAMLET*

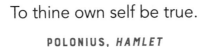

He will give the devil his due.

PRINCE HENRY, *THE FIRST PART OF
KING HENRY IV*

No legacy is so rich as honesty.

MARIANA, *ALL'S WELL THAT ENDS WELL*

The quality of mercy is not strain'd;
It droppeth, as the gentle
rain from heaven.

PORTIA, *THE MERCHANT OF VENICE*

Nothing comes amiss, so
money comes withal.

GRUMIO, *THE TAMING OF THE SHREW*

I would give all my
fame for a pot of
ale and safety.

BOY, *THE LIFE OF KING HENRY V*

Love all, trust a few,
Do wrong to none.

COUNTESS OF ROUSILLON, *ALL'S WELL
THAT ENDS WELL*

Is it a world to hide virtues in?

SIR TOBY BELCH, *TWELFTH NIGHT*

The tempter, or the tempted,
who sins most?

ANGELO, *MEASURE FOR MEASURE*

I have forgiven and forgotten all.

KING OF FRANCE, *ALL'S WELL THAT ENDS WELL*

Pardon's the word to all.

CYMBELINE, *CYMBELINE*

They say, best men are
moulded out of faults,
And, for the most, become
much more the better
For being a little bad.

MARIANA, *MEASURE FOR MEASURE*

Do as adversaries do in law,
Strive mightily, but eat
and drink as friends.

TRANIO, *THE TAMING OF THE SHREW*

Here's a fish hangs in the net,
like a poor man's right in the
law; 'twill hardly come out.

SECOND FISHERMAN, *PERICLES*

———◆———

Striving to better, oft we
mar what's well.

DUKE OF ALBANY, *KING LEAR*

———◆———

We are arrant knaves, all;
believe none of us.

HAMLET, *HAMLET*

BASE INSULTS

All the infections that the sun sucks up
From bogs, fens, flats, on
Prosper fall, and make him
By inch-meal a disease.

CALIBAN, *THE TEMPEST*

How sharper than a serpent's tooth it is
To have a thankless child!

KING LEAR, *KING LEAR*

Frailty, thy name is woman.

HAMLET, *HAMLET*

O, my offence is rank, it
smells to heaven.

CLAUDIUS, *HAMLET*

Let grief
Convert to anger; blunt not
the heart, enrage it.

MALCOLM, *MACBETH*

Wrath makes him deaf.

QUEEN MARGARET, *THE THIRD PART OF
KING HENRY VI*

The cannons have their
bowels full of wrath;
And ready mounted
are they to spit forth
Their iron indignation
'gainst your walls.

KING JOHN,
THE LIFE AND DEATH OF KING JOHN

Were I like thee, I'd throw away myself.

TIMON, *TIMON OF ATHENS*

Get thee to a nunn'ry, why wouldst
thou be a breeder of sinners?

HAMLET, *HAMLET*

A pox o' your throat, you bawling,
blasphemous, incharitable dog!

SEBASTIAN, *THE TEMPEST*

Thou subtle, perjured,
false, disloyal man!

SILVIA, *THE TWO GENTLEMEN OF VERONA*

Thou art the Mars of malcontents.

PISTOL, *THE MERRY WIVES OF WINDSOR*

Methinks she's too low for a high
praise, too brown for a fair praise,
and too little for a great praise.

BENEDICK, *MUCH ADO ABOUT NOTHING*

Though thou canst swim like a duck, thou art made like a goose.

STEPHANO, *THE TEMPEST*

They say there's but five upon this isle:
we are three of them; if th' other two
be brained like us, the state totters.

TRINCULO, *THE TEMPEST*

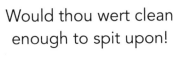

Would thou wert clean
enough to spit upon!

TIMON, *TIMON OF ATHENS*

You bull's pizzle.

FALSTAFF, *THE FIRST PART OF
KING HENRY IV*

You are as a candle, the
better part burnt out.

CHIEF JUSTICE, *THE SECOND PART OF
KING HENRY IV*

———◆———

He has not so much
brain as earwax.

THERSITES, *TROILUS AND CRESSIDA*

———◆———

Your bum is the greatest
thing about you.

ESCALUS, *MEASURE FOR MEASURE*

THERE'S BEGGARY IN LOVE

Then must you speak
Of one that loved not
wisely, but too well.

OTHELLO, *OTHELLO*

———◆———

What our contempts doth
often hurl from us,
We wish it ours again.

ANTONY, *ANTONY AND CLEOPATRA*

———◆———

From forth the fatal loins
of these two foes
A pair of star-cross'd
lovers take their life.

CHORUS, *ROMEO AND JULIET*

THERE'S BEGGARY IN LOVE

Other women cloy
The appetites they feed;
but she makes hungry,
Where most she satisfies.

ENOBARBUS, *ANTONY AND CLEOPATRA*

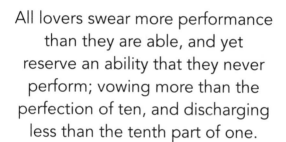

All lovers swear more performance
than they are able, and yet
reserve an ability that they never
perform; vowing more than the
perfection of ten, and discharging
less than the tenth part of one.

CRESSIDA, *TROILUS AND CRESSIDA*

The very instant that I saw you, did
My heart fly to your service;
there resides,
To make me slave to it.

FERDINAND, *THE TEMPEST*

If music be the food
of love, play on,
Give me excess of
it, that surfeiting,
The appetite may
sicken, and so die.

DUKE ORSINO, *TWELFTH NIGHT*

Rich gifts wax poor when
givers prove unkind.

OPHELIA, *HAMLET*

There's beggary in the love
that can be reckoned.

ANTONY, *ANTONY AND CLEOPATRA*

Is whispering nothing?
Is leaning cheek to cheek?
Is meeting noses?

LEONTES ON HIS WIFE'S SUPPOSED INFIDELITY,
THE WINTER'S TALE

Why should you think that I
should woo in scorn?

LYSANDER, *A MIDSUMMER NIGHT'S DREAM*

———◆———

Why then, O brawling
love! O loving hate!

ROMEO, *ROMEO AND JULIET*

———◆———

O, why rebuke you him that loves you so?
Lay breath so bitter on your bitter foe.

DEMETRIUS, *A MIDSUMMER NIGHT'S DREAM*

Love is a devil; there is no evil angel but love.

ARMADO, *LOVE'S LABOUR'S LOST*

Tell me thou lov'st elsewhere;
but in my sight,
Dear heart, forbear to
glance thine eye aside.

SONNET 139

If thou wilt leave me, do
not leave me last,
When other petty griefs
have done their spite.

SONNET 90

This love feel I, that feel
no love in this.

ROMEO, *ROMEO AND JULIET*

The oath of a lover is no stronger than the word of a tapster; they are both the confirmer of false reckonings.

CELIA, *AS YOU LIKE IT*

HOLLOWED EYES AND WRINKLED BROWS

When sapless age, and
weak unable limbs,
Should bring thy father to
his drooping chair.

LORD TALBOT, *THE FIRST PART OF
KING HENRY VI*

———◆———

As they say, when the age
is in, the wit is out.

DOGBERRY, *MUCH ADO ABOUT NOTHING*

———◆———

To view with hollow eye,
and wrinkled brow,
An age of poverty.

ANTONIO, *THE MERCHANT OF VENICE*

I have lived long
enough: my way of life
Is fall'n into the sear,
the yellow leaf.

MACBETH, *MACBETH*

Sir, I am too old to learn.

EARL OF KENT, *KING LEAR*

And as, with age, his
body uglier grows,
So his mind cankers.

PROSPERO, *THE TEMPEST*

Doth not the appetite alter? A man
loves the meat in his youth that
he cannot endure in his age.

BENEDICK, *MUCH ADO ABOUT NOTHING*

I never knew so
young a body with
so old a head.

CLERK READING BELLARIO'S LETTER,
THE MERCHANT OF VENICE

His silver hairs
Will purchase us a good opinion.

METELLUS CIMBER, *JULIUS CAESAR*

But on us both did haggish age steal on,
And wore us out of act.

KING OF FRANCE, *ALL'S WELL THAT ENDS WELL*

He that hath a beard is more
than a youth, and he that hath
no beard is less than a man.

BEATRICE, *MUCH ADO ABOUT NOTHING*

Come kiss me, sweet
and twenty,
Youth's a stuff will
not endure.

FESTE, *TWELFTH NIGHT*

They say an old man is twice a child.

ROSENCRANTZ, *HAMLET*

For I am declined
Into the vale of years.

OTHELLO, *OTHELLO*

To me, fair friend, you
never can be old,
For as you were, when
first your eye I eyed,
Such seems your beauty still.

SONNET 104

PLAY
ON

Let there be no noise made, my gentle friends; Unless some dull and favourable hand Will whisper music to my weary spirit.

KING HENRY, *THE SECOND PART OF KING HENRY IV*

In sweet music is such art,
Killing care, and grief of heart,
Fall asleep, or, hearing, die.

QUEEN KATHERINE, *THE FAMOUS HISTORY OF
THE LIFE OF KING HENRY VIII*

— ◆ —

Play, music; and you, brides
and bridegrooms all,
With measure heap'd in joy,
to the measures fall.

DUKE SENIOR, *AS YOU LIKE IT*

— ◆ —

Give me some music;
music, moody food
Of us that trade in love.

CLEOPATRA, *ANTONY AND CLEOPATRA*

Music oft hath
such a charm,
To make bad,
good, and good
provoke to harm.

VINCENTIO, *MEASURE FOR MEASURE*

Is it not strange that sheep's guts
should hale souls out of men's bodies?

BENEDICK, *MUCH ADO ABOUT NOTHING*

Most heavenly music!
It nips me unto listening,
and thick slumber
Hangs upon mine eyes.

PERICLES, *PERICLES*

To know the cause why
music was ordain'd!
Was it not, to refresh the mind of man,
After his studies, or his usual pain?

LUCENTIO, *THE TAMING OF THE SHREW*

Orpheus' lute was strung
with poets' sinews,
Whose golden touch could
soften steel and stones,
Make tigers tame and
huge leviathans
Forsake unsounded deeps
to dance on sands.

PROTEUS, *THE TWO GENTLEMEN OF VERONA*

'Tis strange that death should sing.

PRINCE HENRY, *THE LIFE AND DEATH OF
KING JOHN*

The setting sun, and music at the close,
As the last taste of sweets, is sweetest last.

JOHN OF GAUNT, *THE TRAGEDY
OF KING RICHARD II*

This music crept by me upon the waters;
Allaying both their fury and my passion.

FERDINAND, *THE TEMPEST*

Mark how one string, sweet
husband to another,
Strikes each in each
by mutual ordering;
Resembling sire and child
and happy mother,
Who, all in one, one
pleasing note do sing.

SONNET 8

Such harmony is in immortal souls.

LORENZO, *THE MERCHANT OF VENICE*

How sour sweet music is,
When time is broke and
no proportion kept!

KING RICHARD, *THE TRAGEDY OF*
KING RICHARD II

Why, these are very crotchets
that he speaks;
Note notes, forsooth, and nothing!

DON PEDRO, *MUCH ADO ABOUT NOTHING*

SPEAKING
DAGGERS

The lady doth protest too
much, methinks.

QUEEN GERTRUDE, *HAMLET*

———◆———

The instruments of darkness tell us truths;
Win us with honest trifles, to betray's
In deepest consequence.

BANQUO, *MACBETH*

———◆———

All that glisters is not gold.

PRINCE OF MOROCCO, *THE MERCHANT OF VENICE*

I follow him to serve
my turn upon him.

IAGO, *OTHELLO*

———◆———

For trust not him that hath
once broken faith.

QUEEN ELIZABETH, *THE THIRD PART OF
KING HENRY VI*

———◆———

The devil can cite Scripture
for his purpose.

ANTONIO, *THE MERCHANT OF VENICE*

There's daggers in
men's smiles.

DONALBAIN, *MACBETH*

I like not fair terms,
and a villain's mind.

BASSANIO, *THE MERCHANT OF VENICE*

That one may smile, and
smile, and be a villain.

HAMLET, *HAMLET*

Will all great Neptune's
ocean wash this blood
Clean from my hand? No,
this my hand will rather
The multitudinous seas incarnadine,
Making the green one red.

MACBETH, *MACBETH*

Do you think, I am easier to be played on than a pipe? Call me what instrument you will, though you can fret me, you cannot play upon me.

HAMLET, *HAMLET*

When our actions do not,
Our fears do make us traitors.

LADY MACDUFF, *MACBETH*

Men's vows are women's traitors!

IMOGEN, *CYMBELINE*

I will speak daggers to
her, but use none.

HAMLET, *HAMLET*

Truth's a dog must
to kennel. He must
be whipped out.

FOOL, *KING LEAR*

Et tu, Brute? Then fall, Caesar.

CAESAR, *JULIUS CAESAR*

How subject we old men
are to this vice of lying!

FALSTAFF, *THE SECOND PART OF KING HENRY IV*

Thy ignominy sleep with thee in the grave,
But not remember'd in thy epitaph!

PRINCE HENRY, *THE FIRST PART OF
KING HENRY IV*

A TOUCH OF NATURE

I have seen a medicine,
That's able to breathe life into a stone.

LAFEW, *ALL'S WELL THAT ENDS WELL*

———◆———

Thou, nature, art my
goddess; to thy law
My services are bound.

EDMUND, *KING LEAR*

———◆———

Our foster-nurse of nature is repose.

DOCTOR, *KING LEAR*

Are not you moved,
when all the
sway of earth
Shakes like a
thing unfirm?

CASCA, *JULIUS CAESAR*

I know a bank where the
wild thyme blows,
Where oxlips and the
nodding violet grows,
Quite over-canopied with
luscious woodbine,
With sweet musk-roses,
and with eglantine.

OBERON, *A MIDSUMMER NIGHT'S DREAM*

Here's flowers for you;
Hot lavender, mints, savoury, marjoram;
The marigold, that goes to bed wi' the sun
And with him rises weeping:
these are flowers
Of middle summer.

PERDITA, *THE WINTER'S TALE*

The rose looks fair, but fairer we it deem
For that sweet odour which doth in it live.

SONNET 54

When daisies pied,
and violets blue,
And lady-smocks
all silver-white,
And cuckoo-buds
of yellow hue,
Do paint the meadows
with delight.

SPRING, *LOVE'S LABOUR'S LOST*

Full many a glorious
morning have I seen
Flatter the mountain tops
with sovereign eye,
Kissing with golden face
the meadows green,
Gilding pale streams with
heavenly alchemy.

SONNET 33

— ◆ —

To seek the beauteous eye
of heaven to garnish,
Is wasteful, and ridiculous excess.

**EARL OF SALISBURY, *THE LIFE AND DEATH
OF KING JOHN***

— ◆ —

One touch of nature makes
the whole world kin.

ULYSSES, *TROILUS AND CRESSIDA*

It is the bright day that
brings forth the adder,
And that craves wary walking.

BRUTUS, *JULIUS CAESAR*

Light thickens,
And the crow makes wing
to th' rooky wood;
Good things of day begin
to droop and drowse,
Whiles night's black agents
to their preys do rouse.

MACBETH, *MACBETH*

Met we on hill, in dale, forest, or mead,
By paved fountain, or by rushy brook,
Or on the beached margent of the sea,
To dance our ringlets to the whistling wind.

TITANIA, *A MIDSUMMER NIGHT'S DREAM*

There's rosemary, that's for remembrance; pray, love, remember: and there is pansies, that's for thoughts.

OPHELIA, *HAMLET*

Thy hounds shall make the
welkin answer them,
And fetch shrill echoes
from the hollow earth.

LORD, *THE TAMING OF THE SHREW*

———◆———

How the poor souls roared,
and the sea mocked them.

CLOWN, *THE WINTER'S TALE*

———◆———

This guest of summer,
The temple-haunting
martlet, does approve,
By his loved mansionry, that
the heaven's breath
Smells wooingly here.

BANQUO, *MACBETH*

WITTY FOOLS AND FOOLISH WIT

Asses are made to bear,
and so are you.

KATHERINA, *THE TAMING OF THE SHREW*

God hath given you one face, and
you make yourselves another.

HAMLET ON WOMEN AND COSMETICS, *HAMLET*

I have a kind of alacrity in sinking.

FALSTAFF, *THE MERRY WIVES OF WINDSOR*

The first thing we do, let's kill all the lawyers.

DICK, *THE SECOND PART OF KING HENRY VI*

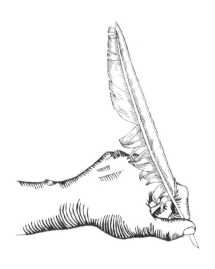

That was laid on with a trowel.

CELIA, *AS YOU LIKE IT*

Light, seeking light, doth
light of light beguile.

LORD BEROWNE, *LOVE'S LABOUR'S LOST*

I do desire we may be better strangers.

ORLANDO, *AS YOU LIKE IT*

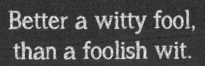

Better a witty fool,
than a foolish wit.

FESTE, *TWELFTH NIGHT*

Misery acquaints a man with
strange bedfellows.

TRINCULO, *THE TEMPEST*

Your abilities are too infant-
like for doing much alone.

MENENIUS, *CORIOLANUS*

Lord, what fools these mortals be!

PUCK, *A MIDSUMMER NIGHT'S DREAM*

There is no more mercy in him, than there is milk in a male tiger.

MENENIUS, *CORIOLANUS*

Brevity is the soul of wit.

POLONIUS, *HAMLET*

———◆———

A little more than kin,
and less than kind.

HAMLET, *HAMLET*

———◆———

When, in the why, and the wherefore,
is neither rhyme nor reason?

DROMIO OF SYRACUSE, *THE COMEDY OF ERRORS*

THE WIT AND WISDOM OF JANE AUSTEN

Max Morris

£9.99
Hardback
ISBN: 978-1-84953-832-9

'Wisdom is better than wit, and in the long run will certainly have the laugh on her side.'

Letter to Fanny Knight

This entertaining collection gathers together Jane Austen's wisest and wittiest quotations. *The Wit and Wisdom of Jane Austen* is a book full of sense and sensibility that's sure to delight all lovers of this great British writer's uniquely humorous and perceptive style.

THE WIT AND WISDOM
OF WINSTON CHURCHILL

Max Morris

£9.99
Hardback
ISBN: 978-1-84953-833-6

'The pessimist sees difficulty in every opportunity. The optimist sees the opportunity in every difficulty.'

This inspiring collection gathers together Winston Churchill's wisest and wittiest quotations. *The Wit and Wisdom of Winston Churchill* showcases his finest hour and is sure to delight all admirers of this great British statesman's rousing and compelling way with words.

If you're interested in finding out more about our books, find us on Facebook at **Summersdale Publishers** and follow us on Twitter at **@Summersdale**.

www.summersdale.com